"This book is one of those rare gems that shares a spiritual practice and, at the same time, manages to give you a spiritual experience.

Dan explains a powerful breathing technique with simplicity, humour, and lightness. You can't help but breathe along with him, and resultantly find yourself in an altered state of mind... open, receptive, and free... which is exactly what he says this breathing technique will do for you! Looking forward to seeing more work by Dan Joy."

Yolanda Barker – writer, yoga
teacher and award winning
documentary filmmaker, author of
„The Breathing Revolution"

"Dan's approach to breathing is joyful and powerful in the sense that it reconnects us to ourselves in time and space. It´s a reconnection to the rawness of just being, and the marvel of the breath as the fuel to the next here and now. His context has that spark of simplicity, and it is an invitation for the journey to presence and groundedness. Thanks for this fresh air!"

José – workshop participant

"It is easy to get lost in all spiritual concepts.

This book helps to go straight to the deepest meaning of all spiritual traditions. It is happening not only through the words but also with the practice you will learn. I am sure that if you give it a go, this surprisingly easy exercise will stay with you for a long time or even for the rest of your life."

Michal Kutzner – open meditation
teacher and life coach

"I LOVED your book, thank you! I found it inspiring, informative and with so much heart. It has changed my relationship with my breath, meditation and ultimately with myself."

Jane Egginton – wellnesss and travel writer, author of over 40 books, yoga teacher, shamanic healer

"I have just finished the book and it felt like I could hear you reading it to me. Telling me the stories and guiding me. The book conveys exactly who and how you are. I loved it. I had forgotten how freeing here and now was."

Kirsty – mum, lomi lomi student

"I just wanted to share my love and gratitude to Dan for sharing the beautiful 'here and now' breathing technique with me. It feels like the missing piece that I've been searching for in calming my mind and keeping my focus on track. I have really struggled with staying in the present during meditations and this allows me to easily bring mindfulness into my life, both when I'm being still in meditation and even when I'm carrying out daily tasks. I will be forever grateful for this, it is simply magic!"

Rachael – workshop participant

"Absolutely BREATHTAKINGLY awesome!!! Wonderful advice and clear guidance on establishing a breath practice that you can adapt to whatever your needs are, spiritual or practical. Highly recommended."

Frëan – retreat centre manager, wizard-yogi

Dan Joy

The Here And Now Breathing Practice

How A Spiritual Cliché Can Become Your Embodied Reality

acknowledgements

I dedicate this book to Dora, my wife.

Of course... there is this part, where I say thank you for the meticulous proofreading, which made sense of many of my too long and complicated phrases[1]. I got it.

(And if there are any spelling mistakes here, in this acknowledgement, it is because you could not proofread this, as it comes as a surprise – we both know how much you like surprises...)

What I more importantly want to say thank you for is something, which cannot really be put into words.

The closest attempts to express my gratitude would be to say:

- thank you for still being – and bearing – with me as I become a better version of myself. "I do my best, gringo!"
- thank you for teaching me those lessons on unconditional love – lessons I am not sure I would have survived with anyone else in this incarnation.
- thank you for sharing with me the gift of your awakening. I see you. And it IS getting easier. Pinkie promise 😊

And now, after disposing of all those wet tissue papers... let's get down to conscious breathing and reading!

---

[1] And thank you for the cover image as well – it was taken by Dora in Burma at Bagan, in February 2020.

Thank you, Wallis, for the amazing illustrations.

They are simple, funny and brought a fresh energy into the evolution of the manuscript.

www.walliseates.com

itinerary

introduction

> "Between stimulus and response there is a space.
> In that space is our power to choose our response.
> In our response lies our growth and our freedom."
>
> Viktor E. Frankl

In this booklet, I will share information regarding a beautiful, simple and powerful breathing practice that became part of my life around the autumn of 2019.

It was an intense period of my life.

As a result of an approximately 3.5 year long coaching process, during the summer of 2019, I was finally able to create some very simple statements and a clear vision about my purpose[2] for the rest of my life.

(Not without a smile, I mention here one of my favourite 14-min Osho lectures you find on Youtube titled: "Life has no purpose". Just for good measure. ;-))

---

[2] My deepest gratitude goes to dr. Balazs Karafiath who was my wonderful coach and guide in this process. If you want to work on your purpose, using the True Purpose method of Tim Kelly, get in touch with Balazs – he is a source of clarity in the field and beyond. www.purposeandplay.com

After a several year long transformational journey, which – without a question – started in 2012 by meeting and dating (again... after a 21-year-long minor pause) my now wife, Dora, and ended up drawing me to live in the United Kingdom, to mark a shift in my perception of the world, of myself and of my journey, I have changed my name to Dan Joy on the 1st of October.

And if that would not have been enough, in November the same year, after failing to become a volunteer for a research of the Imperial College that explored the impact of psilocybin on depression, I decided to take things into my own hands, and after some heroic journeys, I launched myself into my first ever two months long micro dosing experiment with magic mushrooms and truffles.

In the form of an unsolicited insight, first came the first part of the practice, then a few days later the second part... and then it just somehow "clicked" together and became an underlying perspective in my life that a few months later I realised – I can simply call: home.

There is this most beautiful phrase from Ram Dass when he says – "We're all just walking each other home…"

So here is a sweet, old memory from maybe 25 years ago, when I spent a couple of weeks in Ivory Coast, about what discovering home and walking home means for me.

I studied theology and philosophy in France at that time, and I was part of a small international group of people who went for the trip. We were in general referred to as the "French delegation"… even though we were just a bunch of university students guided around in the country by a former protestant priest, who used to be a missionary in the region.

Wherever we travelled, we were welcomed and treated everywhere with amazing love, care and respect, and we also had the honour of being accommodated by local families instead of hostels.

There was one place where we stayed for long, so we had the chance to quite naturally be introduced and involved in one of the rituals of the young people who took care of us... even though they did not call the whole thing a ritual, for them, it was just life happening.

After the daily activities or smaller trips we did, when we got back to the village with our minibus to the church, which was our meeting point, our hosts would send their children to bring each of us back to their homes.

And so that's when it started.
The walking each other home ritual.

To begin with, these local young folks decided who we were going to walk home first. When they picked the first person and location, then all of us, 15-20 people, randomly braced or hand-in-hand, started walking to the address of that family.

The first surprising moment came, when a boy grabbed my hand and just started walking with me like that... and it turned out that boys were walking hand-in-hand or in hugs just as naturally as girls did in their culture.

4

When we got to the address, we all stopped, chatted in front of the house, then the next person and location was decided, and then again – all of us, including the people that we had just walked home – started our next round to walk someone else home.

… and then this just went on and on and on. We decided about the next person and address. Walked them home and then they „joined us" and we started to walk home the following person.

We did these rounds for hours, until it got dark, and then somehow the whole thing came to an end, and people started to really arrive home and the day was over. And then the next evening we did it all over again.

It was beautiful.

The sounds and smells and colours of Africa… combined with these timeless, goalless trips around the dusty roads of the village, round and round the same places, just walking each other home.

I can't stop smiling as I think back… and at the same time I also sigh… as it is just challenging to find the right words to give back the magic of those evenings.

I think this is pretty much how we walk each other home in the sense Ram Dass meant it.

Once I do it for you. Then you do it for me. Then we do it for someone else. We take rounds. We remind each other where home is.

And in a way the whole thing is no big deal, as the Dalai Lama often says, it is just about 'loving kindness'.

At the same time… somehow, you either need to already have been home to be able to walk someone home, or at least you should have a clue how to get there.

The clue that appeared in my awareness during the autumn of 2019, in a way, is nothing new. The important thing is not the intellectual understanding of it, rather the practice of it and the realisations that followed.

ps The reason I decided to make this a zine or booklet was to keep it simple. I knew that I either write about all this for 30 years or take a few deep breaths and make it short and available.

the 30 seconds version

There is this really funny zen story, where a new disciple shows up at the master and asks him:
- Master, how many years will it take to achieve total liberation?
- 10.
- Why...?
- 20.

In other words... the more reactive your mind is, the longer it takes. And by the way, there is no rush either.
Risking that some of the readers will just drop the book after the below paragraph and think they "got it", and more importantly, to give a chance to those that can't read the whole book(let) at this moment in time but might start to practice based on just the below few lines – here is a distilled and condensed version of what this practice is about. So "buckle your seatbelt, Dorothy".

We create the habit to be reminded to be here and now by connecting your inhalation with the notion of "here" and your exhalation with the notion of "now".

As you condition yourself to remember by breathing in to be here and by breathing out to be now, you enter into a positive spiral, where you are either present and aware of your breathing or your breathing will be there as a non-stop reminder to become aware.

Throughout the practice we anchor the focus of our attention in the body, more precisely on the gentle motion of the abdominal area moving up and down as we breathe.

The breathing practice, which organically becomes a habit or our nature, can take place anytime and anywhere, whenever and wherever we don't need to use our mind to resolve a problem or to engage in interaction with other human or sentient beings.

what

The practice is utterly simple: we teach ourselves to be present by using our in-and-out breath as a reminder to do so... or rather to be so.

When we exhale – we remember to be now.
When we inhale – we remember to be here.

To be here and now is to be present. Our breathing is happening in the present. As opposed to the various contents of our mind – our inner chats, the movies we "watch", the thinking about various scenarios or to dos – breathing cannot happen in the future or past: it is always happening here and now.

So if we become aware of it, we inevitably start paying attention to something that is happening right here and right now. In other words, it is a super trustworthy guide (back) to the present.

7

The practice[3] is nothing more or less than teaching ourselves to pick up this habit of focusing on our breathing – whenever we don't need to focus on something else. Which actually is... quite a bunch of time from our linear, 3D worldly time as you will discover.

Sorry. That. Is. It.

In a way, the practice is almost too simple to believe that that is all.

We immediately want to look behind and beyond... to find something more complex, deep or promising.

If you think of it, since our birth, as a child, then teenager, then adult we were not really taught to listen to the quietness. It is a blessing if we had parents, teachers, friends who randomly or deliberately drew our attention to the silence or emptiness or peacefulness of a field, situation or a painting.
Most of the time we pay attention and listen to Something. We are not really "trained" how to listen to Nothing.

The here and now breathing practice is basically learning to have this habit of withdrawing your attention from somewhere or some things, and to deliberately shift and pay attention to your own breathing.

To play with the words, we could say that it is shifting your attention from somewhere to nowhere.

Now and here is nowhere.

As you might discover along your own practice – sorry for the spoiler – this practice will lead you nowhere.

However disappointing it may sound – it will absolutely not get you anywhere.

_____

[3] Sometimes I will refer to it as the "H&N practice" so it would sound more serious. And if you wonder, I did think of it but sorry, I was too coward to use capital P... it was just too much, even for me. The Practice. Auch. That would inevitably get us sliding down the High Priest of The Practice or Certified Practice Master Teacher path.

It is a little bit like the pill scene in the Matrix movie: Morpheus makes it clear that the thing Neo will get is nothing but the truth. No special fun or magical powers, no revelations, no big promises.

Well... same here. And now. ☺

The only promise I would be tempted to offer as a result of this practice is: freedom.

But even with that I would be cautious, so I do my best to define it well.

At the moment, most of us, human beings on this planet, are not free with regards of what we pay attention to. There could be plenty of other aspects of what freedom might mean – regarding opportunities, power, wealth, health, karma etc. – and they all worth to be addressed and explored but in the context of this booklet, I will only focus on one aspect: the freedom to choose what we pay attention to.

To carry on with the perfectly precise images of the Matrix movies, most of us live their lives like most of the people in the matrix. They don't know that they are in the matrix. They don't know that everything they see, hear, smell, touch, feel – is the matrix.

In other words, most people don't even know that there is such an option as not to pay attention to the matrix. As seemingly that is all there is... there is no freedom of choice in what to pay attention to.

In our world, the matrix is a world created by our minds.
And just like in the movie... we pretty much most of the time pay attention to our minds. We don't really have the freedom of choice either.

A large proportion of humankind is stuck in their minds without knowing that it is so and only pay attention to the mind. The mind looking at the mind. We could jokingly say that this is the most exquisite and large-scale form of narcissism one can imagine.

But of course, seen with some compassion, the situation is a bit more tragic than that, as apparently the world created and run by our minds is... well... you know what I mean.

The funny thing about where this practice might bring you is that, as I stated above, it will not bring you somewhere else. It will bring you nowhere. In other words, right where you already are and right when you already are. Sorry. And not sorry.

The shift that might take place could be described by saying that instead of the mind looking at itself it will be awareness looking at the mind[4]. What is... is still all there is. No change. The vision, smell, touch, feelings, sounds will all continue to be the same. Just seen by awareness.

That is all. No more. No less.

Now, of course, there are a few things that come along with this "just".

Pro primo

The first is that the H&N practice will give you a sense of freedom.

Most of the time it comes as a relieve that you don't have to pay attention to your mind stuff. The moments when you return to the present moment, shift and place your attention on your breathing are like fresh air. As the old image goes... it is like waking up from daydreaming or a nightmare and suddenly realising that, thank god, you are present, and you can simply drop the stories, ideas, reflections, inner chats or movies about the past or future – and you can just breathe.
This aspect of the practice is really cool. It is liberating.
In a way it is literally mind-blowing that you can induce this shift in focus any time, there is no one and nothing you need for that, it is

---

[4] To elaborate the poetic curve on this thought, it would be fair and beautiful to say that actually it will be awareness looking at awareness. Jeeez. Now that is what I call infinitely shameless narcissism...

available 24/7, you can feel elevated or apathic, no conditions what so ever. F.awesome.

In the spirit of transparency... it is only fair to mention that sometimes there is zero sense of uplifting freedom in the whole thing, and it is just utterly and disappointingly boring. Yep.

Anyway... the sense of freedom is still there, whether you happen to enjoy it or not. The more you do the practice, the more it becomes a habit, so the more you have the actual experience that you can disrupt your conditioning to pay attention to the mind stuff, the easier it gets.

As after all, our way of paying attention to what and how we pay attention is a conditioned habit. That's it.

Just as we were conditioned to behave in a certain way, we can also condition ourselves to behave in a different way. No rocket science.

Success guaranteed? Well... let me skip to the second thing related to the "just" mentioned above. ☺

Pro secundo

So there is this slightly disturbing aspect of the practice – regarding the one who does it.

To release all rhetorical suspense, and to avoid playing any intellectual hide and seek: if you get on well with your H&N practice, and let's assume you are absolutely successful with it, then there will be absolutely nobody left there to enjoy it.

I know... sounds crap.

Actually, it is not that bad as it sounds – let me explain. As much as it is possible to explain at all.

When I mentioned earlier that one way to describe the shift in perception would be to say that instead of the mind looking at itself, it is awareness looking at the mind – I meant it.

Let's pause here for a second. Anyone before and after me talking about all this have realised that the closer we get to the essence of what we want to talk about, the more impossible it gets.

The language – no matter which one – in its current form is simply not designed to describe "stuff" like awareness or liberation.

That is why at a given point, we just all arrive to similar options: using stories, paradoxes, poems, images. And we know exactly that we will fail... it does not matter, we at least want to fail well. That is the closest we can come to it. I guess now it will come to using a paradox and an image.

Coming back to the above thread – "awareness looking at the mind" means: awareness. Not you. The paradox is that it is true that you and awareness are not "compatible", in other words, it is either you looking or awareness looking. At the same time, it is also true that the "you" that appears to define your current identity, appears in awareness so you are awareness already or awareness is you already.

To come out with a centuries old image from the toolkit: if the "you" is a wave in the ocean, then it is

- at the same time true that the wave is part of the ocean without needing to do anything and
- at the same time it is also true that we can point it out as a separate form and shape we call wave.

So are there any good news here at all? Sure.

The good news is that there is something you can do: whenever you remember, you can realise that you are lost in your mind, shift and focus your attention on your exhalation evoking "now" and on your inhalation evoking "here".

(More about how exactly to do that will come in the next chapter "how".)

In a way, we could even say that you can become more or less successful with this breathing practice: there might be a day or days when – out of your roughly 25.000 thousand daily breaths – you don't even remember that there is such a practice at all and you forget to do it even once, and there might be other days when somehow this is how you wake up and you do it hundreds of times until the day is over.

We might as well say that we don't aim too high and our goal is easy enough, so instead of being frustrated forever with a mission impossible we could succeed with it. We don't go for silly stuff like Total Liberation or Enlightenment, we just simply aim to learn how to withdraw our attention from our mind on a daily basis.

That is all... and that leads us nicely to our bad news.

The bad news is – but actually you might as well discover that this is not such a bad news – that if there is anything happening "beyond" this simple daily habit you might decide to pick up... it is none of your business. There simply is nothing for you to do about it.

Pretty much how the above wave cannot do anything to become the ocean. It is already it.

Using any of these heavy weight, traditional expressions like enlightenment, awakening, shift in consciousness or liberation – we've got rather strictly nothing to do about it. The moment we think we are capable of doing anything about it... we are lost in a cul-de-sac.

As Adyashanti puts it jokingly in one of his talks: waking up is like catching the flu. You can't really catch the flu on purpose. You don't even necessarily know or understand how it happens. All you can possibly do is to hang out with folks who got the flu, give them hugs, drink from their cup... and then there might be a higher chance that you will catch it one day. But even then... you are not doing it.

So the bad news is, by the way, also a liberating news: we don't have to carry the burden of trying to make something happen that is absolutely beyond our scope of understanding and power.

As the slogan of Wim Hof goes: "Breathe, motherf.cker...!" – and the rest will take care of itself. Or not. None of your business. One worry less.

To sum it up: if "you" happen to be absolutely successful with the practice, there will be absolutely no space left for the perspective of a "you", and the perspective of awareness will be absolutely all there is. Which from the perspective of the mind – sucks. But I guess, if you are reading a book like this, you would not mind it that much if that happened.

HERE

how

In this chapter, I will give a few hints regarding how to do the H&N breathing practice, and there is at least one innocent thing that is crucially important in order to avoid becoming simply spaced out: the physical location of our focus.

So far I have only vaguely referred to shifting our attention from our mind stuff to the here and now through our breathing but I have not made it precise what I mean by that?

This is exactly where the spiritual cliché of "being in the here and now" can become an expression that leaves the realm of intellectual abstraction and becomes a feasible, embodied practice.

First things first.
We all have the experience of how chaotic the zapping in our mind can sometimes be. Let's say we have just got up, sitting on the side of our bed, and if we are (un)lucky enough to be aware of it at all, we have the following show going on in our mind:
"Oh gosh... which day is it? I am wondering if the toilet seat will be down or up? ... wow, how cool is that the heating is back. Hm, it must be so boring to fix boilers all your life... Ok, but how about being a FedEx delivery man? Is that any better? Well... maybe if you are dating someone because you had a random chat at the door? That is cool, ha? Make your bed... at least make your bed. You know... the monk and the soldier both said it is important to make your bed. Wow... how interesting... I am somehow not reaching for my mobile phone right away. Monday next week got rather packed with massages, we'll see how it goes. Shit, I forgot to get back to Steph's email... it is getting awkward. What rubbish weather. Well... that is just pure UK autumn, no mistake. I wish I could be a dolphin in Hawaii... playing with humans. Haha... But where is my wedding ring?! I can't believe I can't find it. The last physical object I am attached to. That flower needs some water. Oh dear... how is my father? I've been planning to write to him for ages. Well, good luck with that. Anyway... it would be so cool to visit Tim Cliss next week! Yeah... that would be awesome, to show him the lomi lomi, how the same "message" is coming through this. I hope Dora's retreat will be

uplifting next week with Jim Eaton... she really deserves it. But where is that ring...? I can't wait to continue with writing the booklet!"

This could of course be happening while you are travelling on a bus, participating at a (boring) business meeting, standing stuck in the traffic jam with your car, before falling asleep, having your lunch on a park bench or while making love.

If our mind is not trained to just be still when it is on standby – which is by the way any time when we are not deliberately using our mind to engage with something: an excel spreadsheet, a conversation, fixing the hinge of the door, facilitating a workshop, carrying out a septoplasty surgery etc. – it will automatically react to all the various impulses showing up around us, and if there isn't any or enough impulses around us, then it will entertain itself.

I guess anybody reading this has an experience to some extent of what I am describing here.

The good news about all this is that it is simply a habit. The bad news is that by the time we realise that this is not a particularly useful habit, we had usually invested a huge amount of time and energy into creating this habit. Or to be more precise: we had missed investing time and energy into preventing this habit from creating itself.

As we were growing up and were conditioned to learn various rules and adapt them in so many ways to our surroundings, some of these habits or conditionings were beneficial, some of them neutral, some of them destructive.

One of the important beneficial habits we are often not taught is how to tame or – with an Eastern expression – passivate our minds.

We could say that it should be part of teaching our children how to maintain a healthy mental household: just as sooner or later we expect them to do some chores in our home, equally they are taught in school how e.g. not to throw away rubbish in the yard and similar stuff... In the same way, we should be compassionate enough to teach them how to tame and passivate their minds.

Thankfully, there are more and more schools, home education hubs and other progressive learning environments where meditation and mindfulness practices are becoming part of the curriculum.
As – by the way – that should be the case for non-violent communication, emotional intelligence, mediation, project management, conscious touch, embodiment etc..

But let's come back to our original thread, and see how we can change this useless habit most of us have.

The here and now breathing practice, just like most mediation or contemplation practices, teaches us a new habit of disrupting the thought stream, to withdraw our attention and to shift it to somewhere – now-here... – that is present.

On the one hand, there is no epic discovery here. There are many techniques and methods, in particular the anapana meditation, which use breathing as a focal point of directing the attention to the here and now.
On the other hand, there is a slight conscious development here. To make being in the present a new habit I use the – pretty much similar – tools of two contemporary self-development frameworks: the Silva method and NLP, and suggest to expand the time span of the habit from a dedicated "cushion time" to... basically forever. OK, as long as you breathe.

In a way, of course, they haven't invented the wheel either, but both frameworks point out that there are ways how our mind and our body are more likely to learn something quickly and efficiently if we take into consideration some of their patterns and qualities.

In the Silva method, there is a technique called the "memory peg" – it is using something that is easy for us to remember as a "peg" to hold something we would like to learn to remember. Basically gluing together an obvious colour, number, word or movement with something that we would like to remember.
The most frequent example of this – I am sure most of us have already used something similar to this in our lives – when we need to create a password somewhere and we use our date of birth. Or our own phone number. So instead of learning to remember a randomly chosen "new" code, we chose an existing one – D.o.B. or phone

number – and when we need the code we just simply remember "Oh... it was my date of birth... so it is... ". Easy[5].

And I am sure that there are some folks reading this, who have already used Silva's "three finger technique" as well to remember how "easily and effortlessly" they are going to find an empty parking place. ☺

The "three finger technique" or its cousin, which is called "anchoring" in NLP, both use a functioning principle of our mind-body system. Apparently, if we repeatedly connect a physical movement or sensation with a thought or emotional state, then they will start to glue together, and one will start to evoke the other.

If we really want to put it simply, these are various techniques that build on the Pavlovian-reflex: if there is an intense physical impulse (e.g. ringing a bell when receiving food), which is repeated and glued together long enough with receiving food, then after a while the physical impulse (ringing the bell) in itself can evoke the related state of mind or physical reaction (e.g. salivation in the dogs of the referred experiment without actually receiving food).

It might sound pathetic, nevertheless, it is true that this is how "simply" our human nerve system and memory works. Just ask some of those veterans with PTSD what they might go through when a false fire alarm goes off on the street.

---

[5] I remember when I first had an amazing experience with Dan Millman about 7 or 8 years ago at a lecture he gave at Budapest to a few thousand people to demonstrate how memory pegs work. He told us 20 random words. Repeated it a few times, then asked the crowd how much we remember (we also had to remember them in the right order). There were only a few people remembering all 20 in the right order, most of us got lost somewhere in the range of the first 10. Then he embedded all the words in a funny story... repeated the story a few times and tadah! The majority of the crowd, including myself, remembered all of it and in the right order. It was mindblowing. Actually, I still remember some of the words as of today. We are just storytelling beings... we easily remember and tell stories in order to remember stuff. All the folk singers, bards, storytellers embody this quality of us, human beings.

Tony Robbins explains how he created a simple ritual of a few repetitive words and movements of tapping his chest and clapping to condition himself in order to get himself into his peak state within seconds before going out on stage to run a workshop for several thousands of people.

So how about taking advantage of all this and using our own breath as a memory peg or anchor to remind and redirect ourselves to the here and now? Isn't it cool?!
The single most simple and effortless way you can imagine to be constantly, non-stop, flawlessly reminded to be present and to get out of your mind... whenever it is not necessary to have your focus there. And let me tell you... most of the time it is not necessary. ☺

Isn't it genius?

By now, you might read the phrases I started the "what" chapter of this booklet with a slightly different understanding.
Each and every exhalation will be a reminder for you to be NOW,
and each and every inhalation will be a reminder for you to be HERE.

That is – almost – all.

I will soon start to explore the physical location of the focus as an important aspect of this practice but this is the basis: I condition myself to glue together my breathing out with the notion of now and my breathing in with the notion of here. It can't really get simpler than that.

In – here. Out – Now.

And the more I remember to pick up this habit... the easier it becomes. It really is like a positive spiral and as a matter of fact, you can't really screw it up. You are either present, aware, in the here and now – or you have a built in, irreversible, trustworthy reminder to invite and guide you back.
You might forget about all this... but you will not be able to "turn off" your breathing to not to be there for you as a reminder.

And also... at least based on my experience, I have to admit, this is kind of addictive. ☺

I first went on a 10-day vipassana retreat about 20 years ago, and during the last approximately two decades, I have tried so many mindfulness and meditation techniques, I have been on and off practicing them or not, and when I discovered this one, I was just blown away by the joy over the almost banal, effortless nature of the practice.

I can do this while driving, sitting on the toilet, before falling asleep or after waking up, now, as I am writing this book when I take a pause and wait for the next phrase to show up in my awareness, when waiting for someone or the bus or while making love.
And besides the practical aspect of how I can use basically every second of my life when my mind is on "standby" to do this, I also had a realisation after a few months of practicing.
This method is so cool that maybe I just stick to it and look no further for "something else" and it is just going to be one of those habits I will keep until the end of my life.

Breathing in – here. Breathing out – now.

Initially, to start creating the habit, you might explicitly say "here" as you inhale and "now" as you exhale. Of course depending on whether you are on your own or surrounded by people! ☺
So at the beginning pronouncing the words either out loud or mentally is useful.
However relevant these two words are, just as it often happens with various mantras, if you repeat them long or fast enough, they will lose their original meaning and importance and will just dissolve.
And it is fine. Our goal is not to remember two words... but to be present. The words are just pointers and only can accompany us as far as they can.

Now last but not least, let's crack on with the famous theme of the physical location of our attention during the practice. To sum it up: it is our body.

And as the body is a rather large something in this context... we have plenty of choices. One general rule: whatever you chose to be your point of focus in a given moment – stick to it.

During my on-and-off practice of the various techniques and methods I have tried, I've learned that most of them had a focal point of awareness (not all of them though).

Also, most of them had a fixed point, and some of them – like vipassana – was wondering and moving around with the focus of awareness within the body.

The here and now breathing practice – at least in my case and at this moment in time – has got a fix point to focus on. (Ask me 5 years from now and I might have a different take on this...)

For me, initially, it was around my nose. Based on my former silent sittings, it seemed like an obvious choice. Then after a while, I realised that it was somehow "too close" and "too much up" around my head area... and I wanted to get away from there and its energy.

As I went further down, my second stop was around my heart, the chest area. This was a familiar and beloved perspective. I have had a few series of heart-openings during my life, so I did have an experience of how it is to live life through and with the perspective centred around the heart. Somehow, this time, it did not feel like the right place to be though.

So after a few weeks of the above experimentations, I descended to my tummy area... and that is where the end station was for me. Apart from a few exceptions, basically this is where my attention goes and rests when I do the here and now practice.

Some traditions know about awakenings that take place on the level of the mind, of the heart and of the gut; or call this area the "hara" or the "dan tien". Ram Dass also talks about how observing the motion of the abdominal area is a convenient spot to focus on.

Despite any previous readings or knowledge, I am still not sure what guided and pulled me to come down to that area of my body but clearly there was no other place for me to focus my attention on.

Apparently, this is where most of my existential fears, deepest shames, sense of unworthiness, the lack of trust and (self)confidence reside.
So I was and am breathing in and out from here.

The initial, sad and compassionate realisation was that whenever I landed here with my attention there was stretching and tensing and contraction. As I started to exhale and inhale from and into the area it eased up. Then I wondered away. And then I came back. There it was again... the contraction. Almost as to a little child I talked to my tummy and said: relax, don't be afraid, I am here. Then I am lost in the mind stuff, I realise that it happened, I pull back my attention and I descend. And there it is again... the contraction... I focus and breathe from there and to there. And on, and on, and on.

In – here. Out – now.

The home expands and embraces all of me, everywhere, no escape, no hiding, no spot left out. And no rush. I have a whole life to stay there with my loving awareness.
So it seems... that I am coming home.
And again... words fail to describe the beauty of these paradox movements. I am coming home into this body, into this mind, awareness is coming back home to fully reside here, and takes over with its focus. At the same time, there is an expansion happening that opens up from this body and mind towards and into an infinite and timeless awareness.

On the note of the physical location of the focus of your attention, it is useful to highlight that in general, body sensations are a good guide to find your way back to the present moment if you are lost or unsure.

Breathing, as mentioned earlier, is always happening in the here and now. The best guide.

The second best ones are our bodily sensations, the third group is our feelings – but neither of these are "spotless".

Our mind is a powerful tool, and I guess we all have had experiences how we can evoke certain feelings and moods and even body sensations simply by thinking them into "reality".
We can have a proper headache or contraction in our tummy if we think of a scary exam, which will happen in the future, maybe days or weeks away from the present moment.
We might also remember times when we had an arousal simply by thinking of our beloved and how we spent time together and made love in the past.

31

And certainly, some of us had this funny experience when you remember a dream you had and how you had to quickly pull away your head from a tennis ball flying towards you in the dream... and then you automatically pull away your head in the present moment though you are just sitting in a safe place and simply remembering your dream.

So if we focus on our feelings and bodily sensations, they can sometimes mislead us, but I guess these are rather the exceptions. In general, they are helpful to orient and guide us back to the here and now.

Curiously enough, the "rougher" and "harsher" they are, the less the mind can "imitate" them. A good old fashioned pain or joy is likely to happen in the present moment, even more so a genuine itch, burp, poo, vomit, orgasm or tummy-rumble. ☺ Scuzi.

To sum up this chapter, this is what we do and how we do it, when we do the H&N practice:

- we teach ourselves to connect our inhalation with the notion of here and our exhalation with the notion of now,
- as soon as one of them rings the alarm in our awareness we would disrupt the ongoing thought process and withdraw our attention from our mind,
- optionally, we can pronounce the words "here" and "now" as we breath in and out,
- we rest the focus of our attention on the abdominal area gently moving up and down.

That's it. If we get lost in our mind – and it can happen 3 minutes or 10 seconds into the practice – we just repeat. And that's it. Then if we get lost again... we repeat. And so forth... until we have a phenomena coming up in our life that needs our focus: a conversation with someone, to remember the code of a lock or to find an address.

Actually, after a while you will realise that you don't really have to "stop" being here and now to do any of the above activities but from the perspective of the practice we might say that initially we "let go" of doing it.

Besides, in some precise situations (e.g. above) the good old fashioned compassion is the best guide regarding when to do or not to do this breathing practice.

Your baby crying next to you, your colleague having a break down at the opposite desk, someone being lost at a crossroads... well, these are all situations when theoretically it is possible to just chose to focus on your breathing and your own belly button... but maybe it is just more practical and compassionate to interact and help.

And again... it does not necessarily mean that you are "leaving" the here and now, it just means that you might suspend focusing on doing the exercise.

Mid-term hint: after some months of practice you might realise that of course it is not simply the practice that brings and invites you to be present. ☺

The last thing regarding the "how" is that the process of "remembering" to be present can start anywhere: at your inhalation or exhalation, the motion of your chest or tummy, but it can also be the sound of your breathing. The wake up call can also come in the form of a thought: "shit... what am I thinking of right now again unnecessarily?!" And it can also happen that – sent by a divine muse – simply the notion of "here" or "now" appears in your awareness.

To make it clear: thinking is not our enemy.
What we adjust by the practice is what many of us took up as a useless habit of excessive thinking: it became normal to "be thinking" when it serves nothing and nobody, i.e. it is unnecessary.
At the same time, thoughts are not our enemies either.
Occasionally, we can have very inspiring and smart thoughts, and even some of the above "reminding" impulses can come in the form of a thought: "here", "now", "shit... I am lost in thinking again" – these are all thoughts.

Ramana Maharshi said that sometimes thoughts are like thorns. You got a thorn stuck in your thumb, so you take another thorn to get it out somehow. Once you're done – you throw both of them away.

why

> "Between what I think, what I want to say, what I believe I say, what I say, what you want to hear, what you believe you hear, what you hear, what you want to understand, what you think you understand, what you understand … there are ten possibilities that we might have some problem communicating. But let's try anyway…"

As I mentioned earlier, it is a mission impossible to share in writing what I would like to share, and I am doomed to fail. It is all right. I made peace with it... and set myself to fail well.

The phenomenological part of this booklet was the easiest: to simply describe what I do and how I suggest it for you to do it.

The part about explaining what is the point in doing this breathing practice...? Well, that is where the real challenge lies.

In a way, it would be rather important to get this clear as after all it is important, "why" we should do the practice, yet the first layer of my answer is simply... I don't know.

When I started doing it, there was no mystical or transformational experience that moved me to do it. I just had a couple of insights initially a few days apart from each other, and then it felt so natural to make it part of my life that I was not even questioning what is the point in doing so.

I guess there are things in our lives that just don't have to make "sense".
Or more precisely, it is a question of perspective.

Sometimes we just see a picture of a place and we know that we have to travel there one day. No matter what.

Or we hear just a few seconds of a music and we know that we have to figure out what that piece of music is and get hold of the track or to find out who the author is.
Or we listen to a speaker somewhere and we know for sure that we have to have a one on one conversation with the person.

Regarding the "why" of this practice I would like to leave open the option that from one perspective there is no particular reason to do it. Really. You just either "get it" or not, you feel like "bingo" and it is yours or not.
If this resonates with you absolutely, yet you don't exactly understand why... well, welcome to the club! ☺
Know about the below other perspectives and "reasonable" answers... but you won't need them to feel more relaxed or assured that you are just doing the "right" thing by starting or deepening the practice.

Another perspective of answering the "why" is that the H&N practice is highly beneficial for your body and for your mind. Yep.
As most mindfulness, contemplation and mediation techniques would explain, it is true for this practice as well: focusing on your own breathing functions as a switch. Whatever might be the mood or energy when you start doing it, connecting to the natural rhythm of your breath will de-activate the sympathetic nervous system and activate the parasympathetic nervous system. The first one prepares the body for classic fight-flight situations, while the second one "conserves energy as it slows the heart rate, increases intestinal and gland activity, and relaxes sphincter muscles in the gastrointestinal tract"[6].
This is especially true if you slow down your breathing and start to take deep breaths – but slowing down or manipulating your breathing is not part of the here and now practice.
(My observation is though that without manipulating the rhythm or depth of my breathing in any way, there is a tendency for it to naturally become slower and deeper as I start to focus on it.)

---

[6] Just google it, there is a tremendous amount of info out there about this... The above quote was one of my first hits when I researched the exact terms.
https://www.sciencedaily.com/terms/parasympathetic_nervous_syste m.htm#:~:text=The%20parasympathetic%20nervous%20system%20i s,muscles%20in%20the%20gastrointestinal%20tract.

NOW

A third perspective of the answer would be the whole thread regarding home... and coming home... and in particular coming home into the body.

When I first had a realisation about this perspective, I was crossing the road, and again, the words here and now appeared in my awareness. I pulled back my attention from the actual stream of thoughts, breathing in, breathing out, tears came, tears of joy, of gratitude: what a freedom it is to be able to just breathe and be present... and then I realised – this is home.
That this is my home. Our home. For all of us. To be here and now. Available at all times. I can come here anytime. And even the "get there" part is nothing more than to have my awareness on breathing in and breathing out, which is happening anyway... as long as I am alive... so what could go wrong?
I am either home or I have a non-stop reminder to come home.

So a potential answer to the question of "why" could be to say that it seems that this breathing practice can somehow guide you "home". To feel more home in your body. Or your mind. It somehow enhances the experience of the body-mind package being your home... or in other words, again, to embody your body and to embody your mind.
As a statement: I Am Home.
So there is no messing around here without me... because this is my home.
No destructive patterns... no repetition of unaware stupid stuff... no autopilot reactivity... because I Am Home, I Am Aware and I take care of this body and this mind.
Without becoming too poetic, often the notion of friendship appeared to me as I think of the H&N practice: as if I would become more and more a genuine friend and ally for my own body and mind by simply paying attention to it and being aware of it.

A forth perspective to answer the "why" question would be to address those lovely – fellow ;-) – seekers out there, and to say maybe this practice is just "good enough" to drop the search for something else. It is easy, innocent, simple, you can do it for 20 seconds or 3 hours... and how about this: you can do this until the end of your life.

When I had my first realisation about this perspective, I was in our kitchen, after doing some morning push ups, and again, tears came,

NOW

just sitting on the floor and crying from gratitude... from the relief: I can stop the search. This will be good enough. Like a burden dropping from my shoulders.

The part I can do – I can do that: it's teaching myself to withdraw my attention from the mind whenever it is not necessary to have it there. It is learning a new habit. No big deal. We can all pick up and create habits. Neuroplasticity. Tony Robbins. Blahblahblah. Feasible.

The part I can't do anything about – I don't have to: it's the whole thing about awakening and liberation... it is none of my business. Of course it wasn't ever... but somehow, now, I could just allow myself to be content with the practice, which is just so easy as it is to breathe, and I don't have to worry about the rest.

Best case scenario: one day I get enlightened. Whatever that means.
Worst case scenario: every single day I become a more aware, embodied human being who is present in his body and mind more and more.

These are not too bad options, now, are they...?!

The last and fifth perspective of the answer to the "why" question is, let's face it, that there is a whole story about awakening-enlightment-liberation-shift in consciousness-self-realisation... fill in the dots and use your favourite expression.

If there is such a "thing" – and apparently there is quite a bunch of folks writing and talking about it – wouldn't it be nice to leave at least a tiny bit of a chance that we can do something about it in a harmless way?

Of course... most non-dualistic speakers and teachers, especially the hard core ones, would absolutely tell me off for even entertaining a thought like that, YET.

In one of his talks, Adyashanti mentions that after his 20+ years of teaching, he had to admit that there is a correlation between people having various awakening experiences and the meditation or silent sitting practices these people have been carrying out.

In other words, even though neither him, nor me question the impossibility of "waking yourself up" – for plenty of reasons that I am not explaining here – , apparently more people wake up proportionally from those who do various spiritual practices than those who don't do anything.

Cause and effect connection – no. Correlation – seemingly yes. ☺

Using, again, one of those clumsy images in my desperation to explain this, it is a bit like being struck by a lightning. There pretty much isn't anything you can do to make that happen. Beyond your control.

YET. If there is a huge storm and there is a wide open field and then you decide to run up and down on that field in the storm... there is a higher chance that you are going to get struck by a lightning, isn't it[7]?!

Cause and effect connection – no. Correlation – seemingly yes.

Our simple and innocent here and now practice is rather harmless in that regard: even if you had any dirty intentions and thoughts around doing it in order to achieve enlightenment, the moment you do the practice properly, all similar thoughts will fall away. You focus on your breathing, your tummy going up and down – end of story.

There is a joke that sheds light on our situation quite well, in which an old lady goes to see the GP. Her situation is rather hopeless and so she begs the doctor to at least prescribe something.
So she reluctantly does. The old lady reads out laud the prescription: "mud-pack".
-   And doctor, will that help? – she asks.
-   No – tells the doctor – but at least you will get used to the earth.

You got the gist, ha?

_____

[7] I really love the honesty of Adyashanti – and by the way of so many other folks who woke up and speak about this honestly, like Mooji, Tim Cliss, Jim Newman, Jim Eaton – because it just makes it clear that even though most of our spiritual heros would hihghlight that there is no way from „here" to „there" or from „ordinary" to the „non-dual" state, the same folks would also shed light on their „pre-awakening" journey, and share with us that they have been „searching" like crazy, some of them to the extent of obsession or self-harm.
So yes... there certainly are folks like Eckhart Tolle, Suzanne Segal and many others, who just did get struck by the light(ning), unprepared, unsollicited, some of them having no idea for months or years what had happened to them... but for most of the awakened people we know of – that was not the case.

45

non-duality

Well... I almost thought I can get away without this, but then I realised that after all, it just would not be fair. At least towards some of our readers who don't know too much about this. I mean "THIS"! ☺

And this is where I can definitely only fail with words... so without any further ado let's give it a go.

The simplest way to start with is to first explain that the ordinary perspective most human beings have on life is dual. There is a human being with a name, an identity or a notion of what we call "I" – and then there is the rest of the world, basically "everything else" outside of it.
This duality induces a state of being, which is familiar to most of us, and which is often described as a sense of separatedness: "I" am different than "You", or the Subject of all perceptions is different than the Objects of all perceptions.

Again, in our desperate attempt to describe the indescribable, we return to the good old image of the wave and the ocean.
From a non-dualistic perspective, human beings are like a funny wave that desperately seeks to become the ocean, and is not capable of realising that it is already the ocean – simply because of its strong and seemingly undisputable belief that it is just a wave and separate from the ocean.
Using this image, human beings are already the ocean – i.e. awareness or in a non-dual state – but our belief that we are separate is so powerful that we perceive and experience our belief as reality. Looking from here, a non-dual state is maybe a desirable goal to achieve... yet things don't look so well: do you remember the stories from earlier about the impossibility of catching the flu or being struck by a lightning on purpose? Yeah. 👻

At the same time – to re-introduce some hope – we all have, no exceptions, glimpses of non-dual states. These are those random moments when time stops, our usual boundaries disappear and we expand into something infinitely larger than our usual selves.
We can have such moments while making love, in the flow of running, or doing artwork, or dancing, or using psychedelic substances, or doing holotrop breathing.

Anybody having these moments can confirm that it was not something we did. We might have hoped for it, or prepared ourselves for it, or even prepared circumstances... but it just happened somehow – beyond our control. That state of mind was and is not the cause-and-effect result of any activity we ever carried or will carry out.

So what is the relationship between these moments and the here and now breathing practice?

From a purely educational point of view I must say: nothing. No-thing. Zero.

From a bit less serious point of view: it's like in the above joke with the old lady and the mud-pack.
Will doing the here and now practice help in our desperate situation regarding becoming the ocean?
No. But at least we get used to the water.

embodiment

Yeah. That is a bit like non-duality. Hard not to mention it. Especially as at this point in my life, the two expressions are almost synonyms. At least from a human being's point of view they both point to the same thing.

Embodiment means coming home into your body.

Whatever that means to you.

Beside it being just another sweet and empty spiritual cliché, it can also mean to fully embody your body and mind, to take refuge in the wisdom and presence of this amazing (not-just-a)thing called the body, to surrender to it and – at last – to allow it to take its right place and become our co-creator that it always has been, even if neglected.

For a couple of years now, the name of the excel spreadsheet where I collect and store useful info for my personal life – regarding my health, wealth, stuff to read-do-explore, surprises to arrange for my wife or daughter one day etc. – is called: "embodied self-expression".

Whatever my state of body or mind is... I can use my body, and it can use me to express myself. For me it is like a gradual realisation that you have a best friend – since eternity.

As I am writing this, I know that in a couple of weeks or so I will be a speaker and panellist at The Embodiment Conference 2020... and I have never felt so thankful and proud, as I have never been more aligned with who I am, what I do and on what platform I talk about it.

Focusing our attention to the abdominal area when doing the here and now practice is a simple recognition that whenever there is no need for our attention to be somewhere else, it's best place is to be home and rest as awareness in the centre of our body.

Doing the practice you will soon realise that actually... the body... does not exactly start and end where you thought.

frequently asked questions

What is the "right attitude" for doing the here and now breathing practice?

Ideally, you would have an excitementless, ordinary awareness, similar to when you push a trolley in a shopping centre and you casually walk to the next aisle for the next item on the shopping list.
No rush but not being spaced out either, you know what to do, you have done it already many times, it is almost boring, yet it does need a bit of your attention, as there are other people around, and they might have changed the location of the stuff you are looking for.

On that note – is it possible to do the practice and do something else... e.g. shopping at the same time?

Absolutely yes!
Being present and doing something is not an either-or.
Actually, the whole practice is not the only way to experience being here and now, and I am in no way suggesting that there are no other ways to be present. Of course there are. We can be present in various ways, not just by focusing on our tummy or our exhalation and inhalation.
The practice is just what it is – a practice. A clue. Once you become good at something... you don't need to practice anymore, now do you? 😌
In general, there is a limited amount of info we can handle. If the focus of our attention is on how our abdominal area is moving up and down, we can still do some other things... like pushing a trolley in a shopping mall. Or have a walk. Or we can randomly do it during a long and comfortable conversation. We can also do this together with someone when sharing a "gourmet" hug or when making love.
But in general if we focus somewhere... then we just focus somewhere. In the periphery of our attention – just exactly how our eyes work – we can still perceive things, yet the focus remains the focus.
You'll find a bit more about this under the "Is it possible to overdo this?" question.

49

What do we do with our breathing?

Nothing. No. Thing.
We don't do anything with our breathing.
We don't slow it down, we don't make it deeper. None of that.
As I mentioned earlier, our breathing has got a tendency to become slower and deeper if we pay attention to it but we don't aim to manipulate it in any way.
It is possible, and in some pranayama or yoga practices it is part of the practice – but not for this one.
Here we simply focus our attention on the breathing and use it as an anchor and guide to trustworthily bring us back to the here and now.

Can you overdo this?

Sure, of course!
Like anything else, it can become an obsession or addiction.
In general, especially when it's about human interaction – compassion is a great guide how (not) to do the H&N breathing practice.
If someone is talking to you or is in pain but instead of listening, you just persistently focus on your breathing and how your belly button is going up and down... well, you are actually disconnecting yourself from life, and it will have nothing to do with being here and now.

Which thoughts to pay attention to?

Well... that is the million dollar question. If you got an answer to that question – let me know.
I really don't have a good – especially not short – answer to that.
We do have great and uplifting and creative thoughts sometimes.
We do.
Many of our most inspired actions and interactions are a result of amazing thoughts. Or at least this is how it seems to be happening. I am sharing information now through thoughts.
Yet... it is also true that we simply are conditioned to pay way too much attention to the thinking process that happens in our minds, so we do that even when it is unnecessary or harmful.

50

The reason why yoga, meditation, tantra, contemplation, tai-chi, lomi lomi or extreme sports are "useful" is because they re-introduce a way of being into our life, which is thought-less or when thoughts are either absent or we deliberately don't pay attention to them. So we basically teach – recondition – ourselves to feel comfortable, natural, joyous and safe while ignoring the thinking process.

In my experience though... if you have a healthy, well-functioning, smart mind – it wants to be useful.

Fair enough.

So it only makes sense to find a balance where you have dedicated times of paying attention to your thoughts and use your intelligence and other times when thinking is out of the throne and is set aside.

For me writing books, for example, is one free and "legally permitted" duration when I welcome my thoughts and I deliberately pay attention to them. Even though writing is actually becoming a kind of flow anyway... but these are definitely moments when I don't just disregard thoughts.

For a while, I used to have two types of regular mediation practices: one was a vipassana type mediation, during which thoughts were completely disregarded.

When I realised that actually these deep and peaceful states of mind often resulted in "clear thinking", and really creative and disruptive solutions emerged to some of the problems in my life, yet I was disregarding all of them without exception, I decided to set up another meditation practice.

During this other practice, I still used the same method to focus my attention but I "maintained the right" for myself that if there was a really precious or useful thought, then I would write it down on a sheet of paper. Sometimes I had nothing... sometimes I wrote down a few thoughts.

Both practices need some self-discipline: the first one to be able to disregard the thoughts, no matter how seductive they seem to be; the second one to not to trick yourself and to evaluate every second thought worthy enough to write down... ☺

What if I do it the other way around and if inhalation is now and exhalation is here?

Nothing. It is all right. Experiment.

As for the sound, also for the feeling – for me exhalation is naturally now and inhalation is here. Same in Hungarian – which is my mother tongue – "itt" and "most" just resonate quite naturally with the here and now. And this is how the original insights came as well.

I have confused it many times and I let it to be so, in other words, I am not desperate to change it back the other way... but sooner or later it just always goes back to exhalation – now, inhalation – here.

Can I combine this practice with other techniques?

Theoretically – sure! Go ahead and experiment. Practically – the beauty of this breathing practice is in its simplicity... and especially for an initial period of time, I would just stick with it as it is. If you can.

One thing the mind will sooner or later have "against" this practice is, that it is just too damn boring.

So it will come up with all sorts of ideas – thoughts... – on how to change and amend and enhance it. Basically it will try everything to get you back to busyness by trying to figure out how to make this practice even better.

Innocent, benevolent thought... but it is just a thought nevertheless.

You might discover some new aspects of the H&N practice that I was – and maybe still am – blind to. Let me know if you do so.

And you might just fall for the temptation of paying attention to your thinking... which is not exactly the goal.

Only you will know.

For a few months, I alternatively used the H&N practice and the Wim Hof method. As I was learning the latter and did it randomly during my day whenever I could, so sometimes I had to choose: is it the H&N practice or the Wim Hof method I was going to do?

The Wim Hof method rather drastically changes your state of mind and state of body within a few minutes – no doubt. If you do even just one round properly – 30 quick and deep breaths-holding back-"squeezing" – there is no way you will stay the same as before. Doing two or more rounds would clearly get you high.

(I would definitely not recommend to do it while driving... if you know what I mean. I almost crashed our car once until I've learnt it.)

The here and now practice has no such goal. We simply aim to withdraw attention from wherever it is, and focus it on our tummy rising and sinking – that's it.

Any kind of change in your body or state of mind is a side effect or bonus.

In general, again, I would say: if you really want to go deep with this exercise, give it 3-6 months exclusive time to see what it brings for you.

I have been doing this only for over a year and a half or so – which may sound very short, at the same time, it means lots and lots of hours of practice. Besides other random times, working as a complementary therapist and a part-time pizza delivery guy allows me to use the majority of my working hours to engage with the practice. During these hours I don't have to use too much of my thinking capacity, which could in theory be anything between 20-40 hours per week – depending on how lazy or aware I am.

As earlier mentioned, sometimes I have days when I just haven't even had one conscious exhalation-inhalation... so if the above numbers would give you the false impression that I am a champion of peacefulness or awareness... just ask my wife or daughter or my lovely lomi lomi team.

They would let you know that – as we euphemistically put it sometimes in coaching – there is space for improvement. ☺

If you think of the time of washing your teeth, having a shower, commuting to your workplace, waiting for something or someone, sitting in a traffic jam, all as potential times to practice – it can actually add up to quite a lot of minutes and hours of your day.

Coming back to the question of combing this with other practices, at this point my insight is that personally this is going to be my home base for quite a while. I might try other methods and techniques but this is where I will return. And of course leaving open the option of being wrong – if you are around, please ask me this question again 50 years from now. We'll see.

Can I combine this breathing practice with counting my breathing?

If necessary, yes. That is probably the only in depth exploration I had with combining the H&N practice with other methods.

(Actually I also had some play around saying "I – Am" instead of "here – now" but I dropped it rather soon.)

I have been using the technique of counting 1 to 10 for every exhalation and starting over from 1 once I made it to 10 or when I forgot where I was.

I also used the technique of simply setting a number as a duration of the practice – like doing it for 200 or 300 exhalations. If I got lost, then I always went back to the last number I clearly remembered.

With both techniques, if I pronounce the here and now mentally, then the number would come after the now towards the end of the exhalation.

Inhalation – here...

Exhalation – now... 23.

Inhalation – here...

Exhalation – now... 24.

And so forth.

In general, I used numbers when my mind was more agitated and it was rather challenging to focus. The exercise of counting helped me to get the mind "useful" and "do" something. Sometimes just maintaining the focus on the breathing and the abdominal area is too "thin" or "light" and the mind wonders away more easily.

The counting can occasionally and initially give more "grip" to slow down the system, anchor the attention and then to continue to maintain focus.

Why did you write this booklet?

Well... partly because I was curious what kind of illustration Wallis would come up with for the booklet.

She did absolutely amazing!

Partly I wanted to have a simple, easy to read and grasp guide on how to do this. I am non-native, so this is written in plain, fool-proof English – now that you have read it, you can't ever say again that "you did not understand or know about this"!

Doesn't this practice make you passive?

Nope. Learning how to passivate your mind does not mean that you will become "passive" as a human being.

It is a bit – actually a lot – as if you would live in a house that is just full of noise all the time. Maybe except when you sleep. Apart from that it is just non-stop loud of all sorts of noises.

Let's imagine that somehow you find a magical way to turn off the noise... at last.

Does it mean that you can't sing? Or play music? Or by the way do anything that involves sound?

Of course not. As a matter of fact it might be that for the first time in your life you will properly hear your own voice in your home.

In the same way, having some quiet space in your mind won't stop you interacting or expressing yourself in various ways in life. As a matter of fact, it might be that you finally get a chance to genuinely do so.

Centering yourself in your body through your breathing is not an end station. It brings your awareness fully to the present moment and liberates you to be and do whatever needs to happen through you in a given situation.

Is this an individualistic practice?

Yes and no. Again: question of perspective.

From the perspective of "who does this" – assuming that there is anyone there... – this is a lonely path. No one can do this for or instead of you, which is by the way probably true for all similar methods and techniques.

From the perspective of separation or dualistic perspective the contrary is true: doing this breathing practice you can potentially step closer and closer to realising how your fellow human beings and you – are one.

The ultimate home were we finally arrive is the same home for all of us.

On a more practical level: it is possible to do this practice together with other people just as it is possible to do various types of silent sittings together. Yet, we will have to embrace, again, the paradox similar to the wave and ocean image: even though we can create a community of human beings merging in practising together, they all will be focusing on their own breathing and individual bodies.

On an even more practical level: as I referred to this a few times in the booklet and highlighted at the previous question, doing this practice is not an end station. Neither is it an excuse for not participating in life. Of course... you can use it so but it is not meant to be for that.

It would not be too congruent to now suddenly come up with all sort of magical benefits of the practice when earlier I stated that the only promise I might offer as a result of doing it would be a sense of freedom.

Having said that, in alignment with the opening quote from Viktor E. Frankl – it is reasonable to assume that a more aware, embodied version of yourself is likely to be less reactive and as a consequence to be more patient and compassionate.

Isn't this whole practice just reinforcing the existence of the "I" and its separation at the end of the day?

Well, you know... I don't know. Who does? I mean, really. Who?!

From a hard core non-dualistic perspective of course there is no one to "remember" to be present as you are pure awareness, presence, consciousness, so this whole thing is silliness.
And it's fine... at the same time, it is just a perspective.
From the perspective of a human being we simply do have the experience that we are somehow "lost" in our mind, and in that context "remembering" to get out of it and be present is like suddenly accessing some fresh air, as we are on the brink of suffocating. In the ocean. You know... That Ocean. Which is actually you. Sorry. ☺
Anyway.
If we embrace that we are talking and writing about something ineffable, then we might as well embrace that the whole theme or thread of forgetting and remembering are just clumsy but useful pointings to describe a phenomena that occurs in human beings' lives. No more, no less.

I am still not sure I understand how the practice and interaction with the world around me exactly work at the same time?

Ok, but only because you have asked...
Imagine that you are driving a car.
You realise that it is raining.
You turn on the windscreen wiper – so you could see better.
As the windscreen wiper is turned on and goes left and right or up and down your are not looking at the windscreen wiper and following its motion left and right or up and down with your head... but you are looking ahead at the road. And you do what you need to do as you drive.

Now imagine that you are in a given situation in your life, and you realise that there is a lot of mental noise going on in your head.
You "turn on" the H&N practice – so you could see better.
As you start doing the practice you won't be staring at your belly button going up and down... but you are looking at the situation ahead or around you. And you do what you need to do as you interact.

Capisce?

farewell

There is so much more to be shared. To be precise infinitely more.
But it is not going to come through me... especially not in this form... at least not here and now.
What might happen though is that your body will tell you more and more about the rest as you engage with this breathing practice and give yourself your attention.
It will talk to you in its own language, so if you don't happen to be fluent just yet, get yourself together and start picking it up!
The body will talk to you through feelings and emotions – not sure what is the difference but it sounds good to use both words... – , body sensations, pains and aches and joys and pleasures.
Sometimes it will guide you through simple yes/no type of impulses, sometimes it will tell you more.
Just listen...
... and more and more will reveal itself.

post scriptum

Since finishing the writing, so literally post scriptum of anything above, a few important things had happened that might be important to share.

I have seen the short animation movie of Jessica Wolf about "The Art of Breathing"[8]. Those 9 minutes changed my perspective on my own rib cage, diaphragm, internal organs and breathing in general –

---

[8] http://www.jessicawolfartofbreathing.com/ You need to send her an email... in order to buy the movie.

forever. I can't recommend enough to buy and watch this short video... it's pure bliss.

Then I had a magical structural integration bodywork session with the magical Roger Golten. He gave me a hint regarding how to enhance my posture and suggested that it is less about pulling back my shoulders rather than holding my chest upright.

Thirdly, I have read the book "Breath – The New Science of a Lost Art" by James Nestor[9]. Written in a rather hectic style, it contains an amazing depth and variety of information about breathing.
It highlights the importance of slow nasal breathing – one more reason to engage with a practice that involves conscious breathing.

Another relevant, totally fresh reading experience was the "Recapture the Rapture – Rethinking God, Sex, and Death in a World That's Lost Its Mind" – from Jamie Wheal. There are important chapters about breathwork too but in general I would say that if there is only one book that you are going to read this year – of course... apart mine – then let Jamie's book be the one. Fascinating and grounding stuff.

Last but not least, I went on a few retreats and the central thread of my journeys was around finding refuge and freedom in breathing consciously.
If, before writing this booklet, breathing was important for me, then afterwards, it became the single most important foundation for thriving in my embodied self-expression.

In view of the above, the centre of my focus and my breathing expanded from the abdominal area to include the whole chest.
Et voila, you did not have to wait 5 years until I adjusted my practice.

So... just explore it for yourself and enjoy conscious breathing!

---

[9] Dear Frank, thank you for the recommendation.

... and before you go

If you'd like to get in touch with me then visit

www.presenceinstress.com

for coaching, breathwork or trainings.

Alternatively visit

www.stayintouch.earth

for learning or receiving lomi lomi massage or for cuddle therapy sessions.

If you enjoyed reading then I'd be very grateful if you'd post a short review on Amazon.

All you have to do to leave a few words is to click here, or if you live in the UK then here.

Thank you for your support!

Every second Tuesday at 7.30-8.30pm (London time) there is a Zoom intro-practice-Q&A event. If you'd like to check the dates or join us, click here.

Printed in Great Britain
by Amazon

80406480R00038